BLUFF YOUR WAY IN FINANCE

MICHAEL BECKET

RR
RAVETTE BOOKS

Published by Ravette Publishing Limited
P.O. Box 296
Horsham
West Sussex RH13 8FH
Telephone (01403) 711443

First printed 1989
Reprinted 1991, 1992
Revised 1993, 1995

Series Editor – Anne Tauté

Cover design – Jim Wire
Printing & binding – Cox & Wyman Ltd.
Production – Oval Projects Ltd.

The Bluffer's Guides® series is based
on an original idea by Peter Wolfe.

An **Oval Project**
for Ravette Publishing.

CONTENTS

INTRODUCTION

Finance is a jungle in which even expert hunters are mauled or eaten. Amateurs stand little chance unless they arm themselves with a few weapons. Prod people in the City with the right phrases and they may believe you are too well armed to be consumed.

The novice needs to learn just enough to realise when there is wool in front of his eyes, and to ask questions that will keep the experts feeling they are being watched. For instance, if you ask advice about which shares to buy you are liable to meet condescension and the suggestion that unit trusts may be the wisest move for the small investor. At this point a disingenuous little bluff can warn them to be a bit more careful – something like asking whether the P/E is too low for the sector but the yield below the opportunity cost. That may stop them patronising you.

On the other hand if you ask whether suggested investments provide a return with an adequate net present value, and what discount rate has been used in the DCF calculations and why, you are liable to leave many a financial adviser floundering.

This of course is the essence of all bluff: to hint that you know, but to get the expert sufficiently off his home territory that he cannot be sure whether you are too knowledgeable to tangle with or too sharp to be robbed. With an expert on Rembrandt you steer the conversation to, say, Velazquez (if that is what you know a little about) and he will become ill at ease and wary of flatly contradicting you. With an economist you discuss shop-floor working practices. With City people you discuss economics while knowing just enough not to be caught before the subject is changed.

You do, however, have to take care; the world of finance is itself full of people bluffing for a living, so watch out when these ploys are used on you. An effective counter-play if you suspect you have met a professional bluffer is to insist on his speaking plain English and explaining every term precisely. This is not unreasonable for if they want your cash the least they can do is to speak a language you can understand and not hide behind vaporous double-talk.

If, despite that, they still bury you in jargon, be alert. They may be peddling an idea so obvious, or so false, its fragility needs to be wrapped in verbal fluff to protect it.

So arm yourself with a good enough command of the vocabulary to know when others are bluffing and to provide ammunition for the perfect riposte.

Defensive bluffing, especially on the stock exchange, is to avoid advertising oneself as a sucker. The aggressive bluff however is called fraud and is frowned on if detected and you are within the jurisdiction. In the City you can get away with a lot if you are a smooth unostentatious operator. People will often love you even after you have pocketed their cash. Not to be one of the mugs requires knowledge about what happens and why, so a would-be investor needs to have a firm grasp of the basics if only to show that you know this is not a very serious place and the people in it clever hucksters.

THE STOCK EXCHANGE

The first thing to remember is that you should never allow anyone to fool you into thinking there is something special or mysterious about the stock market or about shares.

Bank notes started as receipts from renaissance jewellers and financiers for gold deposited in their vaults. The receipts were therefore as good as gold but could be traded and exchanged much more easily. The stock market is a logical extension of this.

People are reluctant to lock their investment money into a company forever, so they recover the cash by selling the receipt. This 'market liquidity' makes investors ever ready to stump up, which in turn makes it easier for businesses to raise capital.

That at least is the case for the exchange. It seems not to have noticed that by far the greatest portion of capital used by companies comes either from retained profits or from loans. And some companies got so disgusted by constant scrutiny and criticism they bought back the shares to get rid of the quote.

Seekers after certainty or even predictability are alarmed by the market. As was very succinctly stated: 'Anyone who thinks there is safety in numbers hasn't looked at the stock market page.'

But there is nothing like a quick and easy profit with practically no risk, to tap universal greed: a rash of share options for employees plus privatisations with soaring share prices created 12-13 million shareholders in the past ten years. Some 20% of the adult population now owns a share directly – quite apart from the ones whose pensions and life assurance depend on the stock market.

Like existing shareholders with a little more cash

in their pockets, some of these new capitalists are now wondering if it might be worth dabbling a second toe in the piranha pool, but are deterred by the arrogant effrontery of the jargon, and the high commissions charged by brokers trying to recover from the small saver what they dare not charge the important institutional client.

The important thing to have is confidence, for in fact it is relatively simple, and there are ways of minimising costs. The basic principle is: 'Take as much as you can get and pay no more than you can help.'

The Market

There are two things to bear in mind. Firstly, the stock exchange is no different from a vegetable market (nor are the barrow boys). It is just a matter of learning the share equivalent of the difference between a Cox's Orange Pippin and a Jerusalem artichoke – though it may take a long time before you spot a lemon.

Secondly, the market needs you more than you need it. You can always put your cash into a building society or a sock under the mattress but without your investment market-makers would have to work for a living.

The rules therefore are: keep a grip on your impulse to spend, and be positive. Stockbrokers are like useful hounds; they have to be trained, so will need the occasional firm hand to ensure that they know who is boss.

The stock market employs a number of professionals. When the dealing was personal, the Stock Exchange motto 'Dictum meum pactum' (my word is my bond) meant something, not just because most of them were gentlemen in those days, but because deals worth large sums of money were done on no more than a brief word and a jotted aide memoire in two note-books. Now all is done via computer and such reliance on enlightened self-interest is unnecessary.

Market-makers

Dr Johnson was scornful of jobbers (the market-makers' predecessors) as 'an unnecessary collection of low fellows who speculate in the Funds and are of no benefit to anyone but themselves'. He might have been less charitable about their successors.

What a Market-maker does:

A market-maker buys and sells on his own account and for his own profit. As a result he acts as a buffer to the surges of buying and selling from investors. When all the pressure is to sell, he marks down prices until the sellers are deterred and others smell a bargain. And the other way about.

The market-maker has two prices, say 108-112, which means he buys at 108p and sells at 112p. Prices that are quoted in the newspapers represent the average of these two, the 'middle-market price', just as published currency exchange rates are the mid-point of buying and selling prices.

The difference (between 108p and 112p), known as 'the spread', pays for his risk, his profit and his daily sandwiches. To say the market-maker has a big spread is a comment neither on his belly nor the farm he uses as tax-dodge, but a criticism of his market greed.

It is important to remember that market-makers are the sniff-the-breeze type of instinctive dealers. They have little idea what lies behind names like Shell or Barclays Bank and do not care. From newspapers, the gossip, and a feel for the ways markets behave even when being irrational, they sense the atmosphere and juggle their prices and their dealings.

They used to get very rich indeed but competition, nervous markets and being part of large conglomerates have dented the business. Market problems of this kind are the favourite topic of conversation. It will not be out of place to enquire whether there may be too many market-makers, or to suggest, in a casual way, that there has not been enough growth in turnover to sustain them all, adding that the recent wariness of investors could ensure the difficulty continues. You might ask which may be the next to fall over.

Do not expect to deal with them direct. Market-makers have problems enough without having to cope with every eager small investor ringing up to negotiate each transaction, so they confine themselves to trading with brokers. If you are the British Rail pension fund or the Prudential they may deign to talk to you but if you have under a million pounds in your palm, forget it.

Brokers

Brokers are the middlemen who do the buying on your behalf. As Disraeli said 'It is well known what a middleman is: he is a man who bamboozles one party and plunders the other'.

What a Broker Does

When you telephone a broker he or she swivels round to the computer screen with the Topic service, on which the SEAQ prices pages can be called up. There is no point trying to remember what all the acronyms stand for – the market men haven't got a clue, so why should you. You need only ask whether SEAQ is showing a large volume and whether market-makers are raising their limits.

If it is a popular company like Marks & Spencer or ICI there may be a dozen or more market-makers on the 'page' displaying the buying and selling prices and also the size of 'parcel' in which they are prepared to deal: 1,000 shares or 200,000, for instance. The broker merely looks down the screen, picks the market-maker displaying the best price and, if it is a piddling order, uses the SAEF automatic dealing system for small bargains just by pressing a few buttons. On a larger deal, a bit of horse-trading may take place over the phone especially if the trade is larger than the limit the market-maker has set.

That is all there really is to it. One may be forgiven for thinking that stockbroking requires neither skill nor intelligence, or wondering how they have the gall to demand high commissions.

Major financial institutions have their own SEAQ

terminals and deal directly, small savers are obliged to use brokers. The only fun you can have is to vary your instructions. You can give full discretion to buy and sell on the price and even the timing, or instruct the broker to buy or sell 'at best', or even within set limits.

Chinese Walls

Under the market rules brokers must deal at 'best execution' – i.e. the best price available at the time of dealing. The authorities keep a computer record of prices displayed throughout the day to enable them to check back on details at the time of the deal.

This is to ensure the broker does not bill you for a higher price than he paid, and to prevent the deal being put through the associated market-making firm at a rigged price. It certainly reduces the incidence but sharp lads can usually find a way. At least the range of ways the client can be exploited has been reduced.

The intention is to erect walls between various parts of a company to prevent the broker, market-maker, fund manager, and financial adviser within the one organisation getting an unscrupulous advantage. Why 'Chinese walls' nobody knows, but it is worth observing that the original is highly visible and expensive but failed in its primary task.

Advice

The broker's other function is to advise on investments. Being close to the market and in touch with analysts, a broker is expected to have a better feel for what goes on in the market and why. But do not rely on it. Forecasting is always hazardous, especially of the future. Distrust anyone who claims to predict it: for if they could tell you, they wouldn't, they would just grow rich themselves.

In any case, you will be lucky to find a broker who takes the trouble. For all the loud trumpeting about wider share ownership they are reluctant even to talk to small investors because time is money and fat salaries have to be justified in commission income.

Brokers issue regular circulars on companies or market sectors. These are fat booklets giving elaborate calculations on published figures and regurgitating all that the analyst was told over lunch by the company's finance director. Most professional investors file them in the nearest waste paper basket and the small investors might choose to do the same.

Sensible people know that the big boys received the report long before the small-time spender caught sight of it, and if by chance there had been novelty or sound advice in the findings, they would long ago have acted, ensuring the market is no longer the one described in the report. At the very least, the price will have moved.

But brokers' circulars can be useful on occasions as background information, especially if prepared by one of the better analysts. But keep one thing in mind: most people in broking have never done anything else. They would not know a machine tool if it bit them in the leg; working capital and debtor control are figures on a page; and a supervisor to them is a good sunshade.

To upstage a broker just ask what percentage of the analysts have industrial experience and whether the factory visits entail talking to somebody below the level of managing director. The true answers are zero and no, but listen carefully to the elaborate justifications before you smile knowingly.

If you want to be even more wounding you might ask how many analysts have recently been lost to poaching from other firms. This is snide but reflects the constant musical chairs. If the smug reply is 'none' (rare if the person is truthful) you can trump it by wondering what was wrong with them, or by remarking that it must have cost the firm a bob or two to hang on to them. Never accept disclaimers about this for untruths are told internally about salaries to prevent a mutiny.

However, discussing your 'portfolio' (you must always call your investments a portfolio even if the term covers just the minimum number of British Telecom shares) with a broker can help to clarify your own thoughts. The same applies to their macro-economic forecasts.

Other Animals

There is a curious zoo at the exchange. Not just rats and sharks as unkind people suggest, but bulls, bears and stags. The origins of these creatures are obscure. As good as any explanation is that bulls toss you up, and bears knock you down.

Investors as well as market professionals can be emotional and unrealistic, but can often sense impending fortune or disaster and adjust the share price accordingly. This could account for the strange and apparently random movements in share prices.

Another example is the seemingly perverse mark-down of shares that can occur after a company announces good profits, and vice versa – generally because the news has been already 'discounted', i.e. the market had expected something at least that good and the share price is now looking at the next financial period.

Unexpected, unpredictable and illogical fluctuations in share prices, often in response to rumour and sharp practice, have provoked criticism, not always fairly. Even John Maynard Keynes remarked 'when the capital development of a country becomes the by-product of the activities of a casino, the job is likely to be ill done'. He was a highly successful market investor – often on insider information.

The stock market is a place for betting. The main difference between it and the race course is that if your fancy falls in the 3.30 all your punt is instantly lost, while on the market it can take years before incompetent management and inflation erode the value.

Bulls and Bears

Bull markets have rising prices so people feeling bullish are optimists; bear markets fall and bearish behaviour is gloomy. So for instance a bull of the hotel and catering sector may 'go long' in that sector (pile up a holding of shares). If he is a bear he may 'go short' (sell shares he does not own) – a dangerous gamble based on being able to pick them up cheaper before the time comes to deliver.

The traditional two-week account has fallen victim to computerisation. The system of electronic records which replaced share certificates (what the stock exchange refers to as 'dematerialisation) enables the exchange to have a continuous 'rolling settlement' system instead of fixed account periods.

Market-makers dislike 'bear raids' on a share. This is when a number of dealers sell ostentatiously in the hope of driving down the price so they can nip in to buy shares cheaply before the market realises what is happening and make a profit on their short positions.

To get their own back, market-makers can institute a 'bear squeeze' by marking up the prices. In a panic there may be swift 'bear covering' when the bears who have gone short dash in to buy shares to cover their obligations before the market soars out of reach.

A sophisticated investor might therefore impress with enquiries as to whether a sudden price rise was "just a market ramp" (somebody trying to talk the price up to sell his stake), and a fall was due to a "bear raid".

Stags

Capel Court at the back of the stock exchange used to be called Stag Alley and it was there that the spivs of the last century prospered during the railway mania. First in line for the highly desirable new issue they would dash down the alley and swiftly cash in on their luck.

Similarly nowadays someone who 'stags' an issue of new shares applies at the start with the sole aim of immediate selling, because new issues are always priced low to be sure of their being sold and hence start trading at a substantially higher price: the difference is the premium.

Investment

The stock market has the same thrills as other forms of gambling and can be as expensive and addictive.

What matters is picking the right share. It is exactly like picking a horse, only with different words to cover breeding, jockey, trainer and form. There is even an identical sort of tipster who knows the one that cannot lose. The main difference is that if by some miraculous mischance it is genuine information which comes from the corporate trainer, you become an 'insider dealer' and can go to jail.

Insider dealing (called insider trading in America) is knowing something you shouldn't and doing something because of it. This places one in a quandary, for the whole point of all gambling, especially on shares, is that you reckon to know better the true value than the other half of the trade.

In essence the law says if you have access to 'price-sensitive information' that other investors lack, you have an unfair advantage and hence must not deal. In practice it is easy to spot what is immoral but hard to prove what is illegal. Thus only greedy incompetents who flaunt their activities get caught. But few of them are charged, and even fewer convicted. Faced with ridicule for this the Stock Exchange Surveillance Department is now working hard at monitoring dealings; so dealers are having to be more careful.

On the whole, then, the danger of insider information is not that you will go to jail, but that you will fail to collect the £200. It is far more likely that the gossip is wrong or so stale that it is outsider information only. A shrewd investor is, in any case, sceptical of all information. Ask yourself why somebody should be helping you to make a fortune when those very actions by altering the price could prevent his own success.

There is an old City adage: 'Where there is a tip there is a tap.' This means that someone gives you a tip to buy only if he has on tap a large supply of those shares he is dying to get rid of.

The main lesson is that you can believe nobody. A certain Professor Pepper once advised his friends 'Do not bother to sell your Gas shares. The electric light has no future.' And Irving Fisher, Professor of Economics at Yale, solemnly pronounced: 'Stock prices have reached what looks like a permanently high plateau.' The date was September 1929.

Securities

The word securities is an early example of public relations newspeak since, with rare exceptions, insecurity is their common characteristic. But some are less secure than others.

Companies issue basically two types of paper in return for cash:

- Money on loan, generally at a fixed rate of interest which are called **debentures**, **notes** or **bonds**.

- Long-term money that need never be paid back, and for which **dividends** are paid when profits permit.

For the latter, the company in effect sells part of itself. It is therefore permanent capital and if you hold **ordinary shares** or **equities** (in America this is called common stock) you have not lent money to the enterprise, you are an owner, and the chairman, managing director, et al., are your employees. Remember that, next time the chairman at the AGM cuts off your question about his salary.

Equities is the common synonym for ordinary shares. Holders of shares, as owners, have legal powers to vote on the accounts, appoint directors and auditors and must be provided with a wide range of information. In practice, apathy and ignorance ensure these powers are hardly ever used.

The disadvantage of ordinary shares is that their dividends come out of what is left when everything else has been paid – investment, interest, tax, preference dividends and sugared buns at tea-time. If the company goes down the pan, ordinary shareholders are at the end of the line and seldom get a crumb.

On the other hand if the company thrives, dividends rise smartly (which provides a good income), and as a consequence the share price soars (which provides a nice capital appreciation as well).

Preference shares (just called 'prefs') are more like fixed-interest loans since the dividend is set in advance, and must be paid if the company is in profit.

Blue chips (a term derived from gambling chips in American casinos where the highest value was blue) are those shares of companies considered to be the safest, like the top 30 companies in the FT Ordinary Share Index or the 100 companies in the FT-SE 100 Index.

Alpha, beta, gamma, delta are categories of shares on the SEAQ system. Alpha shares are ones in which there is the most frequent trading and there are stiff rules about dealings in them: market-makers must deal at the price displayed; the deal must be reported to the exchange almost instantly, and so on.

As you go down the line, the willingness to deal and the stiffness of rules diminish until you get to delta where you will be lucky to raise any interest. One of the problems is that gamma and delta shares have a 'narrow market', i.e. there are few shares available, so even a small transaction can trigger a disproportionate change in price.

Below the Greek letters are the riskier shares on the Alternative Investment Market (AIM), about which stock exchange people know little and care even less. These have less onerous requirements about the length and quality of trading record of the company, and the amount of financial information published before they are allowed into the exchange. They tend to attract young and more adventurous companies.

Junk bonds are an American invention. They are used in 'highly leveraged' takeover bids when the bidder has nothing except nerve. This corporate raider issues fixed-interest bonds which are truly junk since unless his bid succeeds he does not have the wherewithal to pay the promised high interest, let alone redeem the bond, and possibly not even then. Like objects in junk shops, they may seem decorative, but are unlikely to be a bargain.

Gilts (short for gilt-edged securities) are not shares but stock issued by the government and therefore reckoned to be safest of all. Being fixed-interest, the price varies with (or to be precise against) the prevailing rate of interest. As bank base rates rise, the price of gilts falls to ensure that a £100 invested in gilts will still remain attractive.

Gilts come in different lengths: 'shorts' are the

short-dated gilts which the government will repay (i.e. when they reach the maturity date) within five years; 'mediums' are 5 to 15 years and 'longs' are the ones that will keep you warm well into the future.

There is one simple rule to remember about the pricing of gilts and indeed all other fixed-interest securities: if the rate of interest on the paper is higher than you could get elsewhere, a dealer may pay more for it, say £105 for £100's worth; and of course not as much if it pays less.

Investors never talk of the rate on fixed-interest securities, but the 'coupon'. This comes from the days not all that long ago when you literally had to snip off coupons fringing the certificate and send them in to claim your dividend.

Fixed-interest stock covers a variety of ingenious instruments. 'Convertibles' here do not mean drop-head but a special sort of stock which can be later swapped for ordinary shares. There are also **prefs** and **loan stock** that give the appearance of brave share buying, but lack most of the risk.

Unit trusts help small investors overcome their fear of risk by spreading their investments over a wide field. But you still have to make a choice from the thousands open to you: whether you want recovery shares, small companies, Far East, America, ethical businesses, electronics, or alternative energy. The units are on a 'bid' and 'offer' basis but the spread is usually wider than for major shares. Unit trusts expand or contract depending on the amount of cash put in by investors.

Investment trusts do not behave in the same way. They are ordinary companies just like any other. The thing that sets them apart is that their sole business is to invest in shares. So you buy them both for their ability to spread the risks and specialism, as with unit trusts, and for their investing acumen.

For some obscure reason the investment trusts quoted on the market sometimes stand at a discount to the actual asset value – the total value of the shares they have invested in. This has tempted bidders which at least can provide an unexpected bonus for the owners. The bluffer will point out that they consistently outperform units, but small investors seem ignorant of this fact. The popularity of investment trusts has gradually increased in recent years and this has not only eliminated the discount on assets for many of their shares, but has led to a steady growth in new ones coming to the market.

Options

If you fancy the chances of a share doing well in say the next six months but have lingering doubts or lack the cash to make dealing worthwhile, you can buy a 'call' option. This entitles you, for a small fee, to buy shares in say BP in 3, 6, or 9 months at a price agreed now.

If you are right and the price rises, the option can be exercised and the shares sold for an immediate profit. If you are wrong, the option is allowed to lapse and only the small option money is lost. Since this is unlikely to be more than 1% of the share price it is a lot less painful than dealing in the shares themselves.

Conviction that the price will plummet in the next few months would prod one into buying a 'put' option which as you would expect provides an entitlement to put or sell the shares at the agreed price at some stage in the future.

If right you buy the cheap shares in the market and exercise the option by selling them at the higher price; if wrong you write off the option cost.

A **double option**, sometimes called a 'straddle', enables you to call or put, but makes sense only if all you guess about the market is that it will fluctuate wildly.

In addition to an outright cheap gamble some people use the market in options to hedge against the need to deal in the shares by providing a safety net. This is obviously a 'secondary market' in the sense of being parasitic on the stock exchange itself. Every flea has a lesser flea: each market spawns another dependent on it.

Traded options

Options in turn have a secondary market built on top. In case you do not want to wait for the option period to expire at the end of 3, 6, or 9 months before seeing if the guess was justified, you can sell the option.

The price of the traded option will depend on how that right to deal is then regarded. For instance, if you have a call option on Consolidated Alaskan Coconut Plantations at 120p in the next two months and they stand at 118p, you might get 7½p if the share is rising strongly enough to make people think it will comfortably top 120p. The price is dependent on how far the rise is expected to continue.

An 'in the money' option has the price below the underlying share, 'out of the money' above.

Judging a Share

Asking "If you are so clever why aren't you rich?" does not work in the City because so many of them are. Unfortunately it does not mean they will make you rich too. The novice needs to know what questions to ask and how to recognise flim-flam in order to discourage it with an apparent sagacity. This is most important when discussing the right share to buy.

To ensure a stockbroker or even your local bank manager takes the job of advising you seriously you have to keep nudging with questions that worry them about just how much you know. You can casually let drop that you "had a look at the quick assets ratio of a few companies but although that seemed fine one cannot tell at the moment whether to buy on fundamentals or to be wary of the toppy look of the charts". (Translation: the financial ratios by which a company is judged made the business look all right but is it right to buy just because a company is sound, though the market looks set to fall: i.e. "I may be a mug but the market doesn't fool me.")

Alternatively you might ponder aloud about the adequacy of the dividend cover.

And it is always acceptable to ask about the management. Brokers hardly ever know, but the question sounds serious. Such comments may well induce a nervous look of respect but you should at all costs avoid getting drawn on the subject. Few can judge managers except by profit, so arguments from ignorance get long and complex. A good quote to remember comes from E.W. Howe: 'Financial sense is knowing that certain men will promise to do certain things, and fail.'

Accounts

Many of the analysts' calculations are based on information in the annual report and accounts of the company. The problem is these can be taken to be a judicious mix of manipulated facts and gibberish.

As accountants never tire of saying, when sued, it is the directors who prepare the accounts – the auditor merely tests whether the information is plausible and the figures actually add up. Auditors tend to let directors get away with murder for if they protest at creative accounting the firm is promptly sacked in favour of a substitute that will not jib at economy with the facts.

If you challenge an accountant on ethics you are likely to get a shifty and uncomfortable defence, especially if you start asking about obligation to be a good citizen and report fraud (auditors are not obliged to tell the police). In any case, the authorities will not bother with cases they might lose. Accountants are likely to change the subject to the profession's achievement in enforcing greater corporate disclosure, even though that has only produced larger audit fees and a greater volume of unreliable figures.

Yield

This is the percentage return you will get if you buy the shares at the stated price. So if the share price rises and the dividend does not, then the yield falls. If the shares cost 50p and the total annual dividend is 10p the yield is 20%. If it really is, be wary. It is a pretty safe rule in life that bargains are rare, and not everyone else in the market is an idiot who has missed the greatest opportunity.

Investors would do well to remember Laocoon's law of improbable generosity: 'Don't look a gift horse in the mouth, but do check for Greek soldiers elsewhere in its anatomy.' If the yield is high, the chances are so is the risk. The obvious question to ask is "What's the problem?"

On the other hand if the yield is very low, the company is well thought of and so the share price may well continue to rise. This might offset in capital appreciation what you lost in yield. Or it might not. Remember this is gambling, and guesswork.

Price/earnings ratio

Another way of looking at the same sort of thing. If you want to show casual command of the subject you can lift an eyebrow and remark "I always think the only really important ratios are cover and P/E." Even the ones who understand may nod sagely.

Cover is the number of times the company could have afforded to pay that level of dividend and is hence a measure of the amount of cash it has available to weather lean periods.

The **P/E** tells you the ratio of share price to earnings. The higher the figure, the greater regard the market has for the company.

A major advantage of this measure is that American and British systems are similar and so transatlantic comparisons can be made directly.

Timing

Your investment timing is at least as important as choosing the right share. Probably more so, for you can make money on shares whichever way they move so long as your timing is right.

One view is encapsulated by Mark Twain: 'October is one of the peculiarly dangerous months to speculate in stocks. The others are July, January, September, April, November, May, March, June, December, August and February.' The stock market has its own adage: 'sell in May and go away.' But this is a hangover of the patterns between the wars and research has shown it to have been unreliable as a guide. A useful conversational gambit is to remark that this maxim has recently usually been wrong.

Charts derive from an observation at the end of the last century by Charles H. Dow (of Dow Jones) that there was a pattern in share price movements. Some of his system is still in use. For instance the 'head and shoulders' pattern – two small peaks with a larger one between them – which indicates a sharp fall.

Poring over these patterns is for obsessives but you ought to know the phrases to keep up with the talk. 'Primary trends' last for years but are interrupted by 'secondary reactions'. In addition phrases like 'support level', 'resistance areas', 'double top', 'channels' and 'triangles' ought to be able to see you through, plus the realisation that the alternative theory to charts is that there is no pattern – the so-called 'random walk theory'.

Beta analysis has absolutely nothing to do with the stock exchange classifications, and precious little with real life. By a complex series of calculations some statisticians purport to show how closely a particular share mirrors market vacillations. A Beta of 1.6 for instance means the share will move 1.6 times as steeply as the market as a whole. Sometimes it does, and sometimes it is recalcitrant. Or as the specialist puts it, the Beta has shifted. Bluffers can afford to be loftily dismissive of the method.

Averaging is the practice of continuing to buy shares even after the price has moved. If you are undeterred by the fall in price and continue buying, the average cost of your total holding will fall. And so might you.

Investment Ratios

You would be well advised to stay clear of this subject because it is hard work and entails hours with company accounts and a calculator. Leave it to the professionals. To make sure they have done the work and take you seriously you might comment "I am totally ignorant of such details of course, but have you looked at the gearing?"

Delphic utterances about the 'quality of earnings' can be useful because, being subjective, one cannot be proved wrong.

You might also ask if the person involved concentrates on 'fundamental analysis' or is a 'chartist'. This means 'Does he look at the company's financial performance or just the share price'. Such a question shows sophistication even though the answer will almost invariably be 'Well, a bit of both, old boy.'

Gearing (known as leverage in America) is the ratio of a company's debts (on which interest varies depending on the prevailing rates), to its share or fixed interest capital. Some think it is shrewd to be 'highly geared' but a company can get badly burned when interest rates rise.

Profitability or **profit margin** is the 'trading profit' (before the deduction of depreciation, interest payments and tax), as a percentage of turnover. A useful guide to a company's competence.

Return on capital is the ratio of profit to the cash used to fund the business. Sometimes called return on assets, or by Americans return on investment. It is worth looking at, if only to ask innocently whether the company might be better off putting its money into a building society.

Asset backing is the when-all-else-fails assessment. If the company went bust, how much would its bits and bobs fetch – things like land, machinery, cash, paper clips and Pirelli calendars, minus of course its debts. Normally the only time anybody bothers about this is during a takeover battle when management suddenly discovers the property is worth millions more than it was the day before. Thus the assets per share are at least double the inadequate offer, and you should forget what the share price was before the bid came.

Acid test (also known as the quick assets ratio) can burn many an investment off the list. The sum of the cash and near-cash (such as readily saleable assets like quoted shares) are compared with the current liabilities (including creditors).

As a rough rule of thumb it is reckoned that a firm is healthy if liabilities are not more than double the cash immediately available; otherwise it could be in trouble in emergencies. (Use sparingly or you might well encounter a City man who asks you to explain.)

Dealing

Until electronics enable you to deal direct, your main task is to find a broker whose fees will not swallow all your profits.

Most stockbrokers find small investors too much trouble and would rather lavish their efforts on the big investors who do not need them. They are not bright enough to work out that if they work well for a small investor, he might become a big one.

You could consult the list with charges that is intermittently published by the stock exchange public relations department, but it is usually out of date. Or you could get a table of charges from the Consumers' Association. Either way, you should bear in mind that it is cheaper to get a dealing-only service (i.e. without investment advice). It is wisest to keep an eye on the personal finance pages of newspapers for the latest league tables of lowest minimum charges.

Takeovers

If you cannot sell your shares, pray for a bid to be made. Big bids escape from the City sections of newspapers and make the front pages, especially if contested as they usually are. They get everybody excited, make merchant bankers rich (which is why they goad clients into such activity), and produce swathes of dramatic clichés from journalists. Newspapers have the excuse that chairmen are similarly afflicted: the bids are invariably dismissed as 'opportunistic, unwelcome and grossly inadequate', and bidders always describe target companies as 'in need of revitalisation'.

Bids often start with a 'dawn raid' during which the bidder's stockbroker starts buying the target's shares like mad at 9.30 am (the stock market's idea of dawn), to pick up the 14.9% permitted under the City Code before the market realises and marks up the shares.

Sometimes it is alleged there is a 'concert party' which sounds like a jolly pierrot show but is merely an unentertaining collaboration between money men to buy shares in a single company. When there is such an agreement their holdings are aggregated for the Takeover Panel rules – for instance you must make a full bid if you hold 30% or more of a company's shares. Watch for allegations of a concert party being instantly defended: good lord no, of course no one is acting in concert, heaven forfend; the various buyers are just part of a 'fan club' (admirers of the corporate raider amassing the shares). They sometimes get away with it too.

A bid is 'hostile' if repulsed, even if the bidder desperately wants to be friendly. If the target dislikes it, but there seems no way of surviving alone, there may be a search for a 'white knight' in the shape of an alternative bidder, preferably someone who will not sack the whole board if he succeeds.

Bid Jargon

Directors lose their jobs when their company is bought so they show greater ingenuity in fending off bids than running the business. But just in case even the most intransigent opposition fails to deter shareholders from accepting a handsome offer, directors have evolved some wonderfully clever ways of saving their own positions.

Here are definitions of some of the more common expressions in bids which are popular in newspapers because journalists love a colourful term even if they do not know what it means.

Poison pill – Corporate suicide to avoid rape. Being taken over is considered a fate worse than death, so directors will swallow such massive doses of debt it knocks the company flat. Corporate necrophilia being unusual, it generally works. But when the would-be rapist goes away, it takes a long time to revive: the defence is sometimes more painful than the menace.

Scorched earth – Toxins of an even more drastic kind. Better distraught than bought.

Shark repellent – Making the company cosy for inept incumbents; fending off predators who might make it efficient by sacking the current lot.

Golden parachute – The directors are about to have a happy landing, whatever happens to the rest of the outfit.

Golden handcuffs – a) The wearer can afford to be rude to the chairman because it would cost a fortune to fire him; b) a means of keeping desirable people from straying and so making the company more highly rated.

Golden handshake – Thank you very much but it is

worth a lot of money to the company to have you around no longer.

Unwelcome bid – The shareholders are delighted, but the board does not like it.

Opportunistic bid – This is probably a good idea but darned inconvenient for us.

Grossly inadequate bid – We cannot think of anything to say but would like it known we do not care for it.

Pac-man defence – The takeover target suddenly turns and tries to eat its assailant.

Reverse takeover – An expensive way to get good management into a big business: a tiny, perhaps unquoted, company buys a much larger one.

Earn out – Linking the purchase price to financial performance (over a number of years) to keep the company's creator at his/her desk long enough to keep the acquired business alive.

Arbitrage

Originally this meant, and in some cases still does, jobbing between markets. Currencies or share prices may get temporarily out of line in different markets and that provides opportunities for the nimble dealer. Buy dollars for pounds in London and immediately do the reverse in New York when the two are out of line and you can emerge with an immediate profit. You can do the same with shares quoted on different exchanges, and in fact anything traded in more than one place.

In New York, freebooters appropriated the neutral term to cover a very different activity. They started by buying into companies with undervalued assets and hence ripe for a bid. Then they decided to ensure their predictions came true by publicising their involvement and so 'putting the company into play' – i.e. nudging potential bidders into action to prevent the good deal eluding them. Finally they made a profit even more certain by buying when they got a leak of an impending bid. This what Ivan Boesky did, and look what happened to him.

Some More Jargon

Here are a few expressions which can come in handy at least for understanding the newspapers.

Bed and breakfast

This is a rather charming term for the practice of allowing you to fiddle taxes legally.

At the end of the financial year one of your shares may be well below the price you paid and ripe for establishing a notional loss to offset against capital gains tax on your successes. But you know it would be silly to sell the shares when it is so down, especially if you have the feeling that prospects are good. Your broker could go through the motions of selling them last thing at night and buying them back again first thing the following morning, paying only a small bed-and-breakfast fee to the market-maker for parking the shares with him overnight. And bingo, your loss has been crystallised as evidenced by the sell contract document.

The index

The way to measure how a market moves is by some aggregate of individual price changes and there is an enormous range of them. In London the two most commonly used are the long-established 'index' (FT Ordinary Share Index) which uses the prices of the 30 largest companies, and ('Footsie') the FT-SE 100 Index which has 100 of them.

In addition there is a bewildering array of FT-Actuaries, indices for a number of industry segments and various overall markets. Even the FT-Actuaries All Share however does not attempt to calculate the average changes of all 4,500 securities traded on the London market.

New York has its Dow Jones, Tokyo its Nikkei, Hong Kong the Hang Seng, Singapore the Straits Times, and so on.

Par value

This is merely the face value of the share. Some are £1, some 5p but the commonest are 10p and 20p. It is of no possible significance other than to the company that issued them.

xd, xc, xr, xa

The letters **xd** next to a share price means ex-dividend so if you buy the share now the previous owner will still get the recently-declared dividend. Similarly **xr** means ex-rights which means you will not be able to subscribe for new shares in the rights issue – a way companies raise money by asking shareholders to buy extra shares at below the prevailing market price.

xc stands for ex-capitalisation, the posh word for a scrip issue which in turn is what happens when a company gives away extra shares for a dividend instead of cash.

Finally **xa** means ex-all if several of these things are happening at once. This means you get just the bare share and none of the recent developments associated with it. Clearly the share price will reflect the presence or absence of these additional benefits.

WORLD STOCK MARKETS

Brokers talk constantly of the global nature of all markets where cash flows through the 24 hours: as Tokyo closes, attention moves through Hong Kong to London and then to Wall Street, whence after a few hours' gap inadequately filled by Chicago and Los Angeles/San Francisco, we are back to Tokyo.

In fact, for general purposes this is nonsense. Institutions might try to spread risks among economies, but just try telephoning your orders through to your broker at 4 a.m. because you've spotted Matsushita has eased a few yen; or even after dinner, to suggest that he sells your BAA shares on the L.A. exchange. To cash in on the continuous world market, it helps to be an insomniac, and to be able to afford a broker who is expensive enough to have a branch beyond Birmingham.

It is worth knowing that if you judge by volume of shares, market capitalisation (value of all the shares at current prices – the expression is used of individual companies as well), or dealing values, Tokyo is number one, followed by Wall Street, with London a long way behind. London tries to rig the statistics by double counting the trade (once for broker and once for market-maker) but it has been rumbled.

For an investor it is appropriate to be awed but puzzled by Tokyo, impressed but wary of Wall Street, and mildly scornful of Europe.

Tokyo

By standards elsewhere, Tokyo is unsatisfactory, not to say shady. This is because:

- insider trading is not just rife but an accepted part of the economic, social and political process
- financial disclosure is inadequate
- the yield is so minimal as to be well nigh invisible
- there are few overseas companies quoted to provide comparison.

Other differences reflect the Japanese character. Instead of sudden shoot-outs so beloved by takeover watchers in Britain and America, the Japanese lack the discourtesy to make someone feel inferior and so avoid bid battles, preferring agreed deals behind the scenes.

New York

Whatever the size of Tokyo, New York dominates European thinking. This is most clearly visible when Wall Street opens with a sudden movement. The London index reacts with such violent sympathy that it can surge off its previous course with a wrenching hysteria.

Wall Street is synonymous in the public mind with New York, but the city is unique in having competing markets.

* **The New York Stock Exchange** (11, Wall Street), also known as the Big Board, which accounts for the vast majority of America's share turnover.
* **The American Stock Exchange** (abbreviated to Amex, and not to be confused with American

Express) which was established in 1793, just one year after its big brother, and which is just a few streets away.

* **NASDAQ** which has a computer-based system for unquoted (over the counter) companies. It was this computer system London bought as the basis for its SEAQ.

The Wall Street equivalent of market-makers are 'specialists' but they do not 'run books' in the way the London people do. They are prepared to absorb some buying and selling pressure by trading on their own account but do not run 'open positions' for long.

American depository receipts (known to their friends as ADRs) are the form in which Wall Street trades in many British companies' shares, especially if they are not quoted in the US. These have the advantage of delaying the discovery of someone building up a stake.

Under British rules:

a) anyone owning more than 5% of a company must own up and declare the stake publicly

b) (under section 212 of the Companies Act) the company itself is entitled to require that any beneficial owners of its shares be identified even if lurking behind a series of disguises such as nominee accounts, Swiss banks, and front-companies in Panama

c) in the absence of convincing answers the shares can be disfranchised, frozen and exempted from dividends, so the owner has no vote, no dividend, and cannot sell them. You may quite often hear about a company 'doing a Section 212 because it suspected a bidder creeping up'.

But ADRs, being bearer shares, have owners who are anonymous with no way of winkling them into the limelight.

The way they are created is by an American merchant bank like Goldman Sachs or Morgan Guaranty buying a parcel of, say, Glaxo shares in London, and locking them into its vaults. Against them in New York it issues a series of notes which can be freely traded and receives their dividends when the owner presents himself to the bank.

The discrepancy in share prices can be explained by the fact that the British like share prices quoted in pennies and thus hold thousands of small value shares; the Americans like share prices in multiples of dollars, and hold small numbers of high value. ADRs tend to be bundles of 3, 5 or even 10 British shares.

Securities and Exchange Commission is the supervising authority for all American securities and corporate activity. As a result the SEC combines the powers that Britain has given to the Department of Trade and Industry, the Bank of England, The City Panel on Takeovers and Mergers ('the Panel') and the whole panoply of self-regulatory bodies under the Financial Services Act. And then some.

For years the SEC was used as the bogeyman to frighten the City into weeding out a few of the more obvious crooked people and practices. Look, said government, the alternative is an SEC and have you seen its documentation requirements?

You will duly express horror at takeover documents being of a size that may not be lifted without endangering some discs, but will go on to point out the SEC did root out Boesky and his tribe of shady insider traders, and it was solely information from those enquiries that burst open the Guinness scandal in Britain.

Europe

A sneer at the rest of Europe is usually in order, but you can raise doubts as to whether complacency in the London market, or the rigour of the controls might not allow trade to drift to another centre. Perm any two from the following:

Frankfurt is only one of eight stock exchanges in Germany but has about half the total turnover because this is where banks congregate, and in Germany banks own businesses. The banks also run a so-called free market and an over-the-counter market but with some reference to the exchange so it is in some ways similar to the USM in London. Related to the economy or to other European exchanges, it is small and sleepy.

Amsterdam houses not only a stock exchange but a number of other markets from diamonds to an options exchange and with **Paris** is rated one of the more serious contenders for being the other European stock market.

In **Zurich** banking, not watches, makes Switzerland tick. It is banks which:

a) organise the law – it is illegal for them to disclose information

b) run the stock exchange.

Banks are the only ones allowed to be members so they have no need for American-style specialists or British market-makers. Since they are the sole members they just trade among each other, ignoring the market floor, then report the totals to the canton authorities who add the figures to the stock exchange statistics. Thus the turnover figures may be viewed with a certain cynicism.

The top ten Swiss companies – three banks, three chemical/pharmaceutical companies, two insurance organisations, Nestlé and Oerlikon – account for over half the turnover. The exchange has a staff of about half a dozen.

Others

Many countries have stock exchanges. But the number of quoted shares and the volume of turnover are so insignificant that they need not detain even the most dedicated.

Hong Kong had a pretty frenetic stock market at the best of times, but with the impending Chinese takeover in 1997 the best of times may well be past, though you would not think so to judge from the booming stock market. Either the locals reckon the Chinese takeover spells the end of money-making and enterprise in Hong Kong and they intend to make the most of what time they have left, or they know something we do not. As a result, the Hang Seng index

Seng index shows ever greater irrational or hysterical fluctuations as it reacts to rumours and opinion.

Singapore is unlikely to require much attention from the amateur bluffer. You may care occasionally to show an admirable global touch by asking about the state of the Straits Times Index as an indicator of sentiment in the Pacific basin.

Sydney has suffered from leading Australian entrepreneurs and corporate jugglers, like Robert Holmes a Court and Alan Bond, tripping over their own tangled finances. As a result some of the financial organisations have succumbed to uncertainty, and the bounce has been taken out of it.

Johannesburg is dominated by gold and mining shares. That is about all you need to know, except that with uncertainty about the political future and the gold price it takes strong nerves and fearless gambling to put your savings into shares there.

OTHER MARKETS

Just as banknotes and shares are tradeable receipts, over 200 years ago London money men realised you can create a secondary market in other things. Like debt.

If a lender needs his money back before the repayment date he could sell the IOU. Bills of exchange, in which a buyer promises to pay the seller in 90 days (or whatever the specified credit period is) can also be sold on, at a discount, to others, like banks. How big a discount you will get on its 'par' (face) value depends on the delay and reliability of the note.

Similar 'securitisation' (turning financial transactions into standard documents to create another market) has become very popular and swarms of 'secondary instruments' have been created. Just about everything can be traded: from mortgage debt, through the level of the stock exchange index in six months' time, to bank deposits.

When every industry succumbs to the Japanese and Americans and every manufactured item is imported, what keeps Britain's finances afloat is the financial services sector. In fact the City is full of very canny traders, some of them so sharp they cut themselves. Wherever there is 'a turn' somebody will be pushing a deal.

There is a tale of a City figure falling overboard in the Indian Ocean but rescued safely after two hours in the fin-infested waters. Asked how he managed to avoid being eaten by the sharks, he calmly suggested it was the forbearance of fellow professionals. Bluffers can point out that this is not entirely accurate. In fact the man would have stripped the hide off eight of them before the lifeboat reached him.

LIFFE

One of the more recent examples is London International Financial Futures Exchange (abbreviated to LIFFE but pronounced 'Life', to avoid sounding like a Dubliner).

The Exchange is worth a visit. From the public gallery you will realise that 'open outcry', as the trading system is called, is an understatement. Liffe traders stand around in groups screaming their heads off, madly semaphoring to tic-tac men by phones round the walls (wearing gaudy jackets for identification) and throwing bits of paper around to keep the show going. The cacophony continues for some 20 minutes and then stops for a break. In this pandemonium, business is apparently done.

The business is trade in future movements of currencies, interest rates or the FT-SE 100 Index. Exporters wanting to protect their income against exchange rate movements can 'buy forward' and so ensure that they get a specific sum when the cash is due. Similarly one can 'hedge' against other financial changes which could damage a business, like interest rate movements or share price changes. The other side of the contract is a speculator taking of risk for a fee.

Money Markets

As long ago as 1350 it was stated that 'money and currency are very strange things. They keep going up and down and no one knows why. If you want to win, you lose no matter how hard you try.'

This is another arena for professionals and those with very large lumps of cash, but it is just as well to know what the terms are if only to discuss comparative interest rates, or mention the markets in passing as if you were commonly trading there.

Certificates of Deposit

In 1966 was born yet another secondary market, the London dollar certificate of deposit, and two years later, sterling was added. Companies with a largish cash pile which they do not immediately need but which they do not want lying idle, put it on deposit. The longer they agree to leave it, the higher the rate of interest. But if the need arrives before the money, the receipt can be sold at a price dependent on the interest rate compared with the alternatives.

Commercial Paper

A short-dated loan note issued by major companies and overseen with a beady eye by the Bank of England, which also sets the rules for security.

Eurobonds

Bluffers should steer clear of this; it is a market for big-time boys and few in the City know much about it except that it's about mega-money and hence important. All you need know is that it allows companies to issue bonds offshore (an American in Europe) and still keep the cash in dollars. Explaining why is irrelevant since few will discuss it. But it might be worth asking why it is the Japanese seem to have taken over the market where once Credit Suisse First Boston was so pre-eminent.

Discount Houses

Finance men point out how useful and efficient a service discount houses provide so bluffers may wonder aloud how it is the rest of the world manages to get along without them. Everything is so delightfully anachronistic about discount houses one instinctively feels reforming zeal will soon sweep them away; later to realise that such illogical and old-fashioned systems are usually better than the systematic inflexibility that replaces them.

The representatives put on their shiny silk top hats to stroll down to the Bank of England. (Note that black toppers were the hallmarks of the plutocrat in Leftist cartoons for about 50 years after their total absence from anywhere but a wedding. Similarly cartoons still have City men in bowlers though none has been seen there for at least 20 years.) From the Bank they buy the whole of each week's supply of Treasury Bills, the short-term money instrument that provides the day to day finance for government. The cash for this comes from banks.

It is a classic case of what a sane money man should not do: they borrow very short (literally overnight to drain surplus cash at a bank), and lend long by committing cash for three months. If they get the sums wrong and run out of money the Bank will help out but at a high rate. It's a dodgy life.

Foreign Exchange (forex)

The City may once have been a bastion of privilege reserved for the scions of wealthy families, but these days in the foreign exchange dealing rooms the accents are not of Harrow, Rugby, Eton or Winchester but of Hackney, Plaistow, Stepney and Whitechapel. The criteria for acceptance, much less success, are:

- lightning reactions
- an ability to do instant complex calculations
- infallible judgment
- limitless physical and mental stamina
- a profound trader's instinct.

A minute movement on one of the screens triggers a flurry of phone calls and deals of hundreds of thousands, possibly millions are concluded in a few minutes. Little wonder that the average foreign exchange dealer is burnt out by his mid-30s. Happily for them, by that time they have generally made enough to retire.

Much of the forex trading – whether 'spot' for immediate delivery or 'forward' – is by companies in international trade trying to 'hedge' against currency movements. Another chunk is to cover institutions' exposed positions. The rest is sheer speculation.

Commodities

One piece of advice has passed into City folklore: if you ever feel like dabbling in the commodities market, take an aspirin and lie down until the feeling passes. Like playing poker, you should not start unless you can afford to lose a lot more than you are gambling. And remember the Hunt family of Texas who lost hundreds of millions of dollars on the silver market.

The seductive charm of trading in commodities is that you buy 'on the margin', meaning you are not asked to put up the full price. The result is like one of those cartoon animals that walks over the edge of the cliff and keeps on walking, until realisation strikes.

To buy say 100 tonnes of 'August' sugar at £120 a tonne you need lay out perhaps no more than 10%, £1,200. It could be more for volatile or high-risk commodities or if the broker doubts his client. If the price moves the right way, say to £150 a tonne over September, October, November, you could multiply the original capital some 24-fold. Heady stuff.

But, if the price goes against you the first thing that happens is the broker asks you for additional margin. Soon after that you may try running for cover and try to limit the losses, which could be enormous if the price say dropped to £60 a tonne, by organising a sell contract. This will not be cheap either but at least you know the extent of the loss.

Similarly if you have a 'bear position' you may well feel naked and if the price rises you will have to keep stumping up and eventually may have to 'close the position' with an expensive contract.

Chicago is the world centre of commodities trading but London has an interesting share: things like rubber and tea which are still traded in and around Plantation House and Mincing Lane, all with their own standard qualities set by agreements in those markets.

Forty-odd commodities are widely traded, and they fall into three basic categories:

1. 'soft' which are mainly food

2. 'hard' which are mainly metals

3. bullion which covers precious metals.

In the first you get cocoa, coffee, sugar, barley, soya bean, tea and wool. In the second aluminium, nickel, tin, zinc, lead and copper. In the third there is gold, silver and platinum. In addition to these sober, predictable things there is wild profusion of the weird and wonderful such as shellac, propane, frozen orange juice, plywood, mercury, coconut oil, cotton, oats and pork bellies.

All deal in 'spot' prices for immediate delivery, and 'futures' for delivery at some specified later date. The two will seldom be the same. Just as the interest obtainable on short and long gilts will differ depending on how people forecast interest rates to move, so discrepancies between spot and futures prices will reflect market price expectations.

Market users are a mixture of the careful manufacturing company steadying future costs (trying to fix how much their raw materials will cost in six months' time) and the wild-eyed gambler attracted by the fact that all the cash does not have to be put up straight away. And, just as in shares, you can 'go short' or 'go long'.

It is fairly well controlled, both in the sense that the traders have the systems sorted and in the sense that producer countries are forever trying to rig the market. Almost every year there are rumours of frost in Brazil in an attempt to push up coffee prices but this is amateur stuff compared with the 'agreements' and 'councils' regulating various commodities.

Unlike OPEC's flagrant attempts at perverting the

market, these bodies try to smooth the wilder oscillations of prices by buying at times of surplus to prevent the price falling further, and then trickling out the supplies during lean years. Note that they seem permanently on the edge of disintegration and some have occasionally been allowed to lapse, but the only one to collapse so far is the International Tin Council whose member countries welched on their promises, leaving traders with total losses said to be over £100m, and creating chaos in the market. Years of litigation failed to shame the governments into honouring their obligations.

London Metal Exchange

When London was the hub of empire, or at least the major trading focus of the world, a number of trading floors were set up to deal in the commodities that might never set foot in Britain. The LME is one of the trading floors and for over 100 years has set world prices for a small number of vital metals by trading among a small number of Ring members. Unlike other markets in London and elsewhere these members make their own contracts – there is no clearing house and no market guarantee.

Copper represents the largest portion of the market but tin, nickel, aluminium, lead and zinc are also traded. As with many commodities market dealing is by 'open outcry' like Liffe, with traders gathered in a ring watched over by a chairman. A bell rings and offers of commodity and money are shouted out until agreement is reached. Not surprisingly, this only happens for five minutes at a time, twice in the morning from 11.50 and twice from 3.30 pm, though there is a small amount of 'kerb' trading afterwards as well. After trading is stopped there is the 'call over' when the agreed price is announced and posted as the official price of that commodity.

The Baltic Exchange

One of several relics of previous centuries that are now hard to categorise, The Baltic Exchange is a strange hybrid dealing in cargo space on ships and aircraft and vessel chartering, but also having a commodities side in grain, oilseeds and soya bean.

Like so many of London's institutions it grew out of transactions across the grimy tables of 18th-century coffee houses, in this case the Virginia and Baltick where captains trading to the American colonies and the Baltic countries used to meet.

Futures and Options Exchange

This used to be called the London Commodities Exchange but changed, perhaps to be able to abbreviate its name to Fox and so use a leaping fox as its logo. As its name implies most things are traded, from oil to wheat. If anyone invites you to participate, check his honesty with the regulatory authorities; and if you are tempted to take part, put your psychiatrist on danger money.

INSURANCE

According to law and market practice insurance has to be done on the basis of 'uberrimae fides' (utmost good faith). In other words, when you are selling your home there is no obligation to draw the buyer's attention to rising damp, woodworm or an imminent by-pass through the garden, but in insurance you must volunteer information which could affect the contract. This may seem a laudably moral view but in practice it is the insurer's best excuse for refusing payment.

Lloyd's

There was a time when Lloyd's was a synonym for commercial rectitude and impregnable finances. An avalanche of huge losses and attendant lawsuits scoured off the gilt, and a series of massive frauds crumbled the gingerbread.

It is over 300 years since sea captains started agreeing insurance with City merchants across the tables of Edward Lloyd's coffee house in Tower Street. Even in the brutal refinery that is Lloyd's new home, its underwriters sit in wooden booths, exact replicas of the high-backed benches in 17th century coffee houses, and the commissionaires are still called waiters.

Lloyd's (the apostrophe is another relic of the ancestry) gets irritated by publicity over insuring a film starlet's legs. Her agent would be a fool not to get simultaneous cover for the rest of her because if anything was damaged, continuing work would be equally hampered. But if you need insurance against something unusual or that has not been insured before there is almost certainly someone at Lloyd's to write a policy, no matter how hard the risk is to assess. This ranges from failure of a broadcasting satellite, to rain on a village fête.

It is run like a gentlemen's club though they have reluctantly allowed in non-gentlemen, like foreigners and women, when they needed the money. But you still need a proposer, an introduction to a member's agent and an interview before they condescend to accept your money.

Members (called 'names') include a number of peers and celebrities. It is worth getting hold of the massive Blue Book to find names to drop. However many a sleek rat has been heading for the shore as Lloyd's accumulated losses of some £8½ billion in the space of about 5 years. Some of the gap they left has been filled by corporate members and it would take a rich, brave and risk-addicted individual to join these days. Those who think they know the convolutions of the insurance cycle can get the buzz of membership without the risk by buying shares in one of the quoted corporate members. But that becomes merely an alternative to other shares. Those who go against the prevailing view and wish to become individual members will need unencumbered wealth of at least £250,000 as collateral, against which insurance is written by the underwriter. You are then encouraged to enrol in a variety of syndicates such as marine, non-marine, aviation, and livestock.

If you are seriously thinking of joining, you may care to remember that if the losses are great enough they can, in the traditional Lloyd's phrase, come at you for your last gold cuff-link. However, any sensible person without unlimited resources takes the precaution of buying 'stop loss' insurance to set a ceiling on the pay-outs. What is more, in the initial years most people restrict their involvement until they have started to build up a cushion of reserves. Always ask whether the rates for stop loss are at a reasonable level at the moment.

One major advantage of Lloyd's remains. You use the same cash twice over for an income. Investments such as shares, gilts, etc. on which there is already a yield and capital appreciation, can be used as money at Lloyd's against which to earn a second income.

If you want to remark on the rows and scandals at Lloyd's you can start with a list containing Savonita, Howden, PCW, Moran, Outhwaite, Warrilow, Sasse – not to mention the LMX spiral. You are safe to mention this last: few people know it stands for London Market Excess of Loss much less begin to grasp how it lost a few thousand members millions of pounds.

The Rest

Not even the most inveterate City and finance bluffer could, or would, be expected to know much about the rest of the insurance market. It is useful to be able to throw out the odd statistic, like the fact that around half the world's insurance originates in the US and a substantial additional portion is arranged in dollars, or hint darkly about the incursions of the Japanese.

You can also ask whether on-screen broking is likely to undermine both Lloyd's and all the other traditional markets and indeed end London's supremacy. The answer will almost always be emollient and reassuring and it is in order to raise a quizzical eyebrow.

FINANCIAL REGULATION

Stanley Baldwin's attack on the press is often turned against the City. He said the papers were aiming at 'power without responsibility, the prerogative of the harlot through the ages' (at which the Duke of Devonshire exclaimed 'That's done it – he's lost us the tarts' vote').

The criticism of blind self-interest is often accompanied by a parallel attack on the City for 'short-termism'. Try to avoid taking sides because much of the argument is inconclusive and getting involved only makes enemies for no purpose. Apart from which you may benefit from the short-termism of your pension fund portfolio manager.

Institutions are accused of just pulling out of questionable ventures and walking away when their knowledge and financial muscle might rescue a precarious business. When they do intervene they are accused of throwing their weight around and meddling in management though they know nothing about industry.

If you are drawn into one of these debates the useful tactic is to ask whether the view opposite to that which is being promulgated has any validity. If short-termism is the topic, complain about:

a) institutional inability to help companies over the long haul they need

b) concentration on horizons far too short for manufacturing.

And point out that critics of short-termism are usually the first to berate investment managers for failing to come top in a six-monthly league table of performance.

If long-termism is being advocated, suggest that long term investment could be said to be short-term investment that has gone wrong.

The Bank of England

Much of the Bank's rôle is as ambiguous as the promise by the chief cashier on bank notes to pay the bearer, but it is known to do several things:

- it runs the country's money (admittedly partly on orders from the Treasury)
- it supervises the City
- it intervenes in the currency markets to stabilise sterling against too disorienting (and disoccidenting) movements.

Thus a precipitous fall will be countered by buying sterling, and vice versa. The nice, if surprising, thing about this is that the Bank makes money out of the transactions. Fortunately in recent years it has been asked only to make the movements gradual, and not as previously to push water uphill.

Knowing what the Bank does enables you to make glancing references to differences of opinion with the Treasury on monetary policy. "Heard the Governor is in favour of using M3 rather than M0 as the criterion" is a useful line, especially as few can remember what the different definitions of money supply mean and the Bank is generally far too shrewd to admit disagreements, even when they are obvious.

Regulation is vague and informal. The suave bluffer will make a knowing reference to the Governor's eyebrows when discussing regulation. The Governor is the head of the Bank and although he has an iron fistful of wide-ranging legal powers, the tradition has been that all of it is hidden in a velvet glove: a gentle hint that a certain practice, a take-over, a person, is not wholly to his liking.

This is the area of British life that most closely approximates the Japanese way of running business with subtle suggestions. From the stock exchange to Lloyd's, from the banks to the commodities businesses, the Governor has his eyes and ears out there. The Bank has been caught out more than once but has averted a number of dangers in ways that elsewhere would be considered unacceptably covert, undemocratic and high-handed.

The debacle surrounding the collapse of BCCI and Barings has dented the Bank's reputation but has not removed its powers. The Governor still has the right to decide in banks (as the Department of Trade and Industry has among insurance companies) whether the people in charge are 'fit and proper' for the task. Since nobody has ever officially defined this, you could say that perhaps someone fit and proper would be one who is able to run up three flights of stairs and not swear at the effort involved.

The Financial Services Act

The enormous complexity of the Financial Services Act was imposed by government because it wanted to protect a few silly people from the consequences of their own folly – 'Warning: careless investment will damage your wealth.' There are always the gullible who are too greedy to realise a high return carries high risks. Because a small number refused to ask sensible questions about investments or bought gold bricks in the Strand, all investors must now fund the regulatory procedure – to the tune of over £200m a year. The Act imposed such stringent and onerous burdens of disclosure and conduct that the City had Sir Kenneth Berrill sacked from chairmanship of the Securities and Investments Board (SIB) for having the impudence to try implementing it.

Instead there is now a streamlined but much more understandable system of self-regulation, with each sector policing itself. The idea of 'set a thief to catch a thief' would appear a good one, but so far it seems to be more concerned with tiny firms failing to file returns on time.

The numbers being robbed in ways which the Act is intended to prevent means that the effect is bound to be small though the cost large. Half the City groans at the red tape and the other half smiles knowingly. You should make noises of cynical disbelief that any of it is working. A spectacular set of fines of many insurance companies for switching people into duff pensions and other misdemeanours has jerked many of the companies awake and they have even started supervising what their salesmen say.

You need to know the outlines of the mechanism only. The Securities and Investment Board heads the packs of City watchdogs, and there are five organisations under it:

- The Financial Intermediaries Managers and Brokers Regulatory Association (FIMBRA)

- The Life Assurance and Unit Trust Regulatory Association (LAUTRO)
- The Securities and Futures Association (SFA)
- The Investment Managers Regulatory Organisation (IMRO)
- The Personal Investment Authority (PIA)

With such catchy names it is little wonder they are known by their initials.

To stir up dissension, ask whether Lloyd's is better off being outside the Act and hence the SIB's invasive requirements, or worse off in view of the massive pile of regulations and bye-laws it had to bring in as the price for independence.

The Panel

The City Panel on Takeovers and Mergers is a curious organisation. Set up at the instigation of the Bank of England which was getting a mite anxious about the piratical way bids were excluding small shareholders, its only powers derive from an agreement among banks and stockbrokers to support it.

Over the years it has compiled the City Code as guidance. It can also intervene in specific cases and issues its own judgments. Curiously nobody knows how much legal power and privilege attaches to these lofty decisions since they have hardly ever been tested in court. This odd position of making its own rules as it goes along, rather than being restricted by courts and legislation, has some considerable advantage: the

Panel can act quickly and informally.

For instance, it can slam stable doors almost faster than horses can bolt, whereas the legislative system would require a parliamentary committee to review briefing the architect about constructing a new stable, and probably redesign the horses as well. So far only one person has openly defied the Panel. This was a man called Jim Raper and stupidly the Panel forgave him, so he went and did it again.

The European Union

There has been much talk about the single European market, especially the wonderful way it will free financial services. The correct riposte to such twaddle is a contemptuous snort.

Since there is little immediate prospect of agreement about the harmonisation of taxes (income, corporation, inheritance tax, excise duties, VAT, etc.), there can be no abandonment of financial restrictions. So for all practical purposes (common European currencies, a common central bank). You can regard the EU as jeux sans frontières. But keep an eye on cross-frontier takeovers because they will be increasing in preparation for whatever increased freedom is hammered out.

Last Refuge

The last refuge of a bluffer is honesty. Bluff the truth and nobody will believe you. In extremis therefore one should look a financier or City expert straight in the eye and say "I am afraid you will have to excuse an ignorant country boy, but I know nothing about money. Can you explain all that in words that even I can understand?"

This will instantly label you as shrewd but modest; the type to watch. If you also interpose with a remark like "I am sorry to be so dense but surely the prospective yield would be a good indicator of a risk/reward ratio. Or have I misunderstood?", they may well treat you with caution verging on respect, but will talk straight English. Which of course, was the whole object.

THE AUTHOR

Michael Becket learnt what little he knows about finance by having to explain it to others. This he does in the columns of *The Daily Telegraph* City pages, a job he came to by the circuitous route of lathe operator, kitchen porter, market research interviewer, advertiser, exhibitions organiser, and the Civil service, which is as good a way as any.

He runs his own publishing house, Flame Books, which specialises in financial guides for the layman, to which this book would provide a useful introduction. The list includes: *How the Stock Exchange Works* by Norman Whetnall in its sixth edition; *How to Protect Your Investments* by Barbara Conway in a revised edition; *Value for Money Insurance*; and his own *Economic Alphabet*.

His latest book is *Office Warfare*, an executive's guide to tactics for winning. He also writes freelance for anyone else who will let him, which has enabled him to give up his non-executive directorships.